Spiders Are Not Insects

WITHDRAWN

By Allan Fowler

Consultants

Robert L. Hillerich, Professor Emeritus,
Bowling Green State University, Bowling Green, Ohio;
Consultant, Pinellas County Schools, Florida

Lynne Kepler, Educational Consultant

Fay Robinson, Child Development Specialist

CP Children's Press®
A Division of Grolier Publishing
New York   London   Hong Kong   Sydney
Danbury, Connecticut

Project Editor: Downing Publishing Services
Designer: Herman Adler Design Group
Photo Researcher: Feldman & Associates, Inc.

Library of Congress Cataloging-in-Publication Data

Fowler, Allan.
   Spiders are not insects / by Allan Fowler.
     p. cm. – (Rookie read-about science)
   Includes index.
   Summary: An introduction to the spider, an eight-legged creature,
not to be confused with the six-legged insect.
   ISBN 0-516-06054-6
   1. Spiders—Juvenile literature. [1. Spiders.] I. Title. II. Series
QL452.2.F68   1996
595.4'4–dc20   96-39673
                                          CIP
                                          AC

hunting spider

You can find spiders almost
anywhere. Some spiders live
in hot, humid rain forests.

tarantula

Others live in hot, dry deserts.

They live in water and
woods, trees and gardens
— and in people's homes.

house spider

Not many animals have
been around as long
as spiders.

Spiders are not insects.

They belong to a group
of animals called arachnids.

Arachnids have eight legs.
Insects have only six.

spotted fishing spider

Arachnids do not have wings. Insects do.

ant lion

hairs on spider leg   jumping spider

Spiders use hairs on their
bodies to sense the world
around them.

milkweed longhorn beetle

Insects sense things with
feelers, called antennae,
that grow on their heads.

Some spiders are so tiny
that you can hardly see them.

crab spider

And some are big enough
to eat birds and mice
and frogs.

frog-eating spider

Mexican red–legged tarantula

The biggest ones belong
to a family of hairy spiders
called tarantulas.

Most spiders are
poisonous, but only a
few kinds are dangerous.

Spider bites can hurt — so
it's best not to touch them.

Only two spiders in
North America are very
dangerous to people:

the brown recluse spider . . .

brown recluse spider

and the female black widow.

female black widow spider

If you see a spider marked with a red hourglass — keep away from it!

You don't want a black widow to bite you.

Female spiders are usually more poisonous than males — and bigger.

Spiders can move quickly.

Some baby spiders can travel through the air.

They cling to silk threads that are blown by the wind. This is called ballooning.

The silk comes from the spiders' own bodies. All spiders produce silk.

net-casting spider

Many kinds of spiders use
their silk to spin webs.

Different kinds of spiders weave webs of different designs.

tunnel spider

Webs are sticky. An insect that lands on a spiderweb becomes trapped.

Monarch butterfly caught in web

garden spider and dragonfly

Then the spider may swing on a thread of silk toward the insect . . . inject it with poison . . . and eat it.

Sometimes spiders use their silk to wrap up a trapped insect to eat later.

garden spider and grasshopper

bird spider (tarantula)

Spiders that don't weave webs are called hunting spiders. They go out looking for their prey. Tarantulas are hunting spiders.

jumping spider

So are jumping spiders,
which attack insects by
jumping on them.

Some spiders even eat other spiders.

golden silk spider

garden spider

Spiders are not easy
to like.

But spiders do help people
by eating insects that are
harmful to plants or
those that carry disease.

Words You Know

Arachnids

jumping spider

black widow spider

tarantula

Spiderwebs

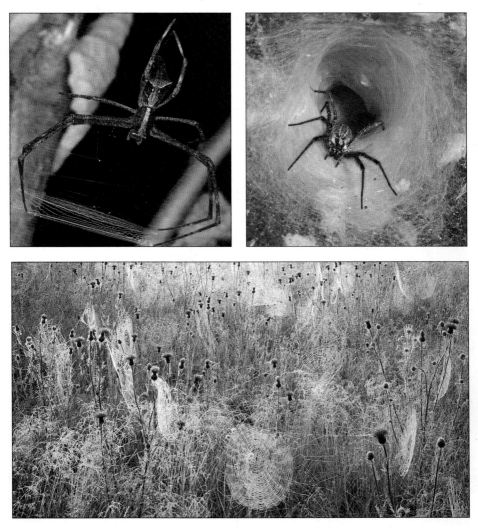

Index

About the Author

Allan Fowler is a free-lance writer with a background in advertising.
Born in New York, he lives in Chicago now and enjoys traveling.

Photo Credits

SuperStock International, Inc. — ©L. Fantozzi, cover; ©A. Gransden, 4;
©L. Jernigan, 24; ©Tom Murphy, 28
Animals Animals — ©Michael Fogden, 3; ©Richard Shiell, 5; ©Richard K. La Val,
12; ©Klaus Uhlenut, 19, 31 (top left); ©Stephen Dalton, 26; ©Patti Murray, 27
Visuals Unlimited — Kjell B. Sandved, 7; ©David M. Phillips, 9 (inset);
©Richard Thom, 15
Tony Stone Images, Inc. — ©Gay Bumgarner, 8; ©David Ochsner, 11; ©Larry
Ulrich, 20, 31 (bottom); ©Steve Taylor, 30 (top)
H. Armstrong Roberts — 9 (large picture), 21, 23, 31 (top right); ©W. Talarowski, 22
Valan Photos — ©Pam Hickman, 10
Tom Stack & Associates — ©David M. Dennis, 13, 30 (bottom right); ©John Cancalosi, 25
Photri, Inc. — 16, 30 (bottom left)
COVER: Garden spider